GUMBO YA YA #5

Denise Alvarado

Carolina Dean

Melony Malsom

Alyne Pustanio

Oskar Yetzirah

Creole Moon Publications

Prescott Valley · New Orleans

Gumbo Ya Ya #5 2014 is published by Creole Moon Publications, Prescott Valley, AZ. 86312, USA. Copyright © 2014 Denise Alvarado, All rights reserved. Photographs and illustrations copyright 2014, Denise Alvarado or are in the public domain. Individual articles are under copyright of their respective authors.

ISBN-13: 978-1497390638 (paper)
ISBN-10: 149739063X (paper)

Primary Category: Social Science/Customs and Traditions
Country of Publication: United States
Publication Date: 3rd Moon 2014
Language: English

CREOLE MOON

Publications

Table of Contents

About Gumbo Ya Ya

Welcome to the 5th edition of Gumbo Ya Ya Conjure Art-zine! As with previous editions, the content of this issue covers a wide gamut of topics from Voudou possession to conjure in the barrio to goddess worship. We are always looking for articles and workings, formulas and spells and invite the reader to submit ideas and articles for publication.

No rhyme, no reason—just because. That's our motto!

Have comments or questions about this zine? Feel free to email me at gumboyaya@creolemoon.com

Brightest blessings,

Denise Alvarado

Editor in Chief
Creole Moon Publications

Email: dalvarado@creolemoon.com
Website: www.creolemoon.com
Blog: conjureart.blogspot.com
Facebook: facebook.com/hoodooandconjure
Fan Page: facebook.com/AuthorDeniseAlvarado

OFFICIAL LEGAL HOOPLA

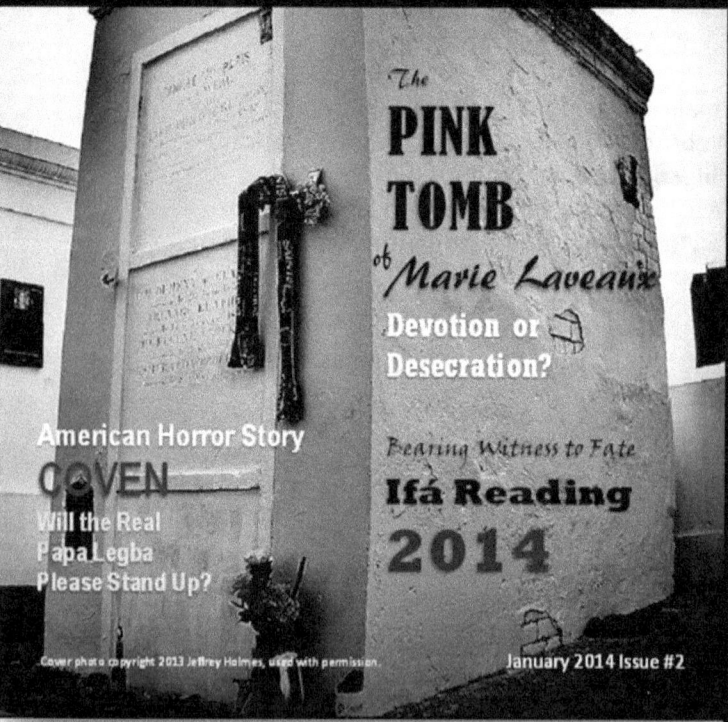

GUMBO YA YA
BACK ISSUES!

ALL FREE DIGITAL DOWNLOADS!

Formulas & Spells

Prayers & Blessings

Saints & Spirits

Louisiana Conjure

Hoodoo & Rootwork

Creole Recipes

West African Recipes

History & Information

Conjure Tips

Tools & Supplies

Herbs & Roots

Stories & Folklore

Choice Moments

Quotes

New Orleans Voudou

And more!

creolemoon.com/zines-ezines.htm

Spells & How They (Sometimes) Work

by Carolina Dean

Spells. Workings. Jobs. These are terms used in Hoodoo to describe acts of magic which are performed out of one's own needs in order to achieve a goal. They are performed for virtually any conceivable purpose including, but not limited to, the following:

- Prosperity
- Health
- Protection
- Love
- Controlling Another
- Sexual Desire
- Justice
- Banishing Evil
- Enhancing Fertility
- Employment& Steady Work
- Cursing
- Success
- Domination
- Blessing
- Death
- Cleansing
- Confusion
- Obtaining Justice
- Gambling Luck
- Reconciliation

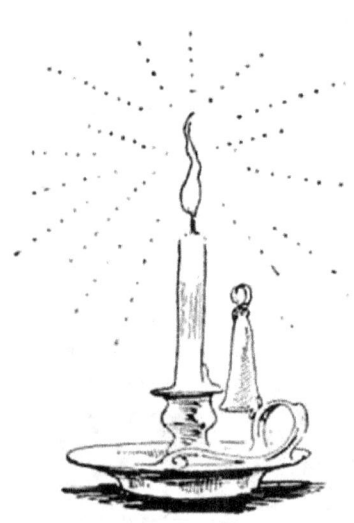

Essentials for Successful Magic

There are certain basics to learning to practice magic that must be understood and mastered as much as possible in order to practice successful magic. While there is something to be said about choosing a mode of magic, obtaining the correct materia magica, and observing times---there are also four basic essentials that will serve your greatly in your magical endeavors. Following is a summary if these four basic essentials.

1. **Knowledge is Power.** It is important that you know yourself and your own limitations; however, it is equally important to continue to advance yourself in order to continue growing and evolving as a spiritual being in a physical existence. While Hoodoo is a very practical form of folk magic, it is continually evolving and changing. For this reason, you can study for a lifetime and never learn all there is to know about Hoodoo. Nonetheless, knowledge in and of itself is not enough. Knowledge must work in conjunction with belief. Belief is the absence of doubt---an unwavering faith in the knowledge that you will have that which you desire. Without such belief, your spell may fail.

2. **What You Dwell on Inwardly, You Manifest Outwardly.** The mind is a fountainhead of untold power which we are only beginning to understand. It has the ability to manifest anything that you desire, and it will manifest that which your thoughts dwell on. If you tell yourself that you are sick, then you will not be healed. If you believe that you are not worthy of love, then you will never find love. This is why we, as folk magicians, speak so often of cleansing ourselves of evil in thought, word, and deed. When we learn to think and act positively, we can manifest the positive things in life for which we yearn.

3. **What Goes Around, Comes Around.** This is both a spiritual axiom and a scientific law. Most folks are familiar with the basic concept of Karma from Eastern Esoteric Teachings which basically states that the law of cause and effect plays a central role in determining how one's life should be lived. Most folks interpret this as what you do (for good or ill) to another person will be done to you as well. Examples of the concept of karma can be found in the Christian Bible such as Proverbs 26:27 ; Galatians 6:7 ; Matthew 26:52. You may have heard it before in school, only it went "for every action, there is an equal and opposite reaction." As we have seen, this is not only true for our actions but our thought as well. Therefore, before performing a spell or working it is very important that a divination be performed in order to determine the probability of

success or failure to avoid any unforeseen negative consequences, and to make any necessary changes to one's plans. This is, however, not to say that in certain circumstances that negative spells such as curses cannot be performed at all. Instead, this means that you must determine if the curse in question is justified (again via divination), or else it may return to you. In any case, most folks often perform an act of cleansing, such as a hyssop bath, after having delivered a curse via magic in order to remove their sin.

4. **The Magic is Inside You.** Herbs. Roots. Candles. Flannel Bags. Dirt. Silver Dimes. These are just a few of the items that can be found in a spiritual practitioner's magical collection. However, it is very important to understand that these items are simply tools. The power does not come from them, but rather it is channeled from the connection between your spirit and the Spirit of the Divine as found in all things. Without a connection to Spirit, you are simply going through the motions.

Why Spells Fail

Anyone who practices magic will tell you that, beyond a shadow of a doubt, magic works. We know it works because if it didn't work those who practice it would not continue to do so. The problem is that it doesn't always work or at least not in the way one originally intended - which begs the question why do spells fail? In my experience, spells fail for one or more of four reasons. They are:

1. **Human Error.** This is a common reason among beginners. It usually occurs when the wrong correspondences were utilized, there was a lack of focus and/or conviction during the spell, an inability to make a spiritual connection with the Divine, or health reasons such as physical illness, depression, or the use of alcohol or drugs which impairs the individual. If your spell fails due to human error, then the answer is to go back and repeat your spell using the correct correspondences, maintaining better focus, and so forth.

2. **Disregard for Tradition.** While not a religion in and of itself, Hoodoo incorporates aspects of religion and has over time developed certain rules which one is expected to follow in order to practice magic successfully. Beginners often come to Hoodoo with preconceived notionsa bout how Hoodoo should and should not be practiced based on incorrect information or their experiences with other magical traditions. Failure often results when folks try to change the rules to suit them rather than change their behavior to suit established practices. Examples of disregard for tradition may include failure to properly pay a spirit in exchange for its grave dirt

or allowing another person to see or touch your mojo-bag. Blatant disregard for traditional rules is not only disrespectful, it is intolerable. To continue to do so may have dire spiritual consequences for the offender. If you have angered a spirit by not properly paying for its goods or services, then that spirit must be appeased with offerings and sincere prayers for forgiveness. If your mojo bag was seen or touch by another then it should be refreshed or re -made as need dictates.

3. **Not Meant to Be.** A spell may fail when we petition Spirit for something that either: a) we are not meant to have; b) what we ask for somehow interferes with our spiritual plan; or c) is not justified (in the case of a hex or curse thrown at an enemy). If a spell is not meant to be, then there would be definite signs along with way before you even cast the spell; that is, if you have performed a divination beforehand. If not, signs may come in the form or dreams or omens. Such signs should not be ignored because Spirit is trying to tell you that you are treading down the wrong path and divination can help steer you in the right direction. For example, you may be trying to cast a love spell on a certain person but, for whatever reasons, the signs say that your spell will fail and that you will not have him or her. Instead your signs may advise you to cast a spell to attract someone with the qualities that you admire in this person instead.

4. **Direct Opposition.** Though it is rare, it does occasionally happen that another practitioner is working against you for any number of reasons. They may have a grudge against you, they may have the same goal as you (i.e. working to attract the same job or love interest) or they may be working on behalf of a client who has paid them to bind and/or cross you for these or other reasons.

As in the last example, if you are regularly performing your divination or seeking signs then direct opposition will be revealed to you in some manner. If it occurs that another practitioner is working against you, then a series of cleansing and reversing work will be in order to avail yourself of their spells and bindings. If the work against you is especially powerful, then you may have to fight back with even stronger spells in the form of your own curses directed at your opponent.

Spells are ritual acts of magic performed to achieve a specific goal such as obtaining love, health, money, or conferring protection. Spells often fail for a variety of reasons. Some of these reasons may include human error, disregard for tradition, asking for something that is not meant to be, or direct opposition by another spiritual force. In order to perform successful magic, you must foster a connection to Spirit, firmly believe in yourself and believe that you can have what you desire. Support this with positive thoughts, words, and deeds and hold firm to the knowledge that what you send forth will come back to you.

About the author: Carolina Dean is a Witch, a Rootworker, a Magickal Craftsman, and a Gifted Reader Born in the Deep South. He is the assistant editor for *Hoodoo and Conjure Magazine* and has written articles for *Witches Hour Magazine, Hoodoo and Conjure Quarterly, Hoodoo and Conjure Magazine, and Gumbo Ya Ya.* He is the co-author of the *Hoodoo Almanac 2012* and *Hoodoo Almanac 2013 Gazette* (with Denise Alvarado and Alyne Pustanio).

Website: www.carolinaconjure.com
Blog: http://carolinadean.blogspot.com
FB Fan Page: www.facebook.com/carolinadeanfanpage
Twitter: www.twitter.com/carolina_dean

****

Aromatic Hyssop Cleansing Bath
by Denise Alvarado

"Purge me with hyssop, and I shall be clean."

The above passage is probably the most referenced statement relating to hyssop since the word was originally written in the Bible. The use of hyssop in cleansing makes sense given the heavy influence of the Bible on modern conjure. To make an aromatic cleansing bath with hyssop, boil a handful of hyssop leaves and flowers along with a handful of rue in a gallon of spring water. Allow to cool and strain out the herbs and set aside. Add the herbal infusion to a warm bath. Light a white candle and anoint with hyssop spiritual oil and set on the edge of the tub. Tea lights or votive candles are ideal for baths because they burn quickly. Get in the tub and pour the water over your head seven times, and recite Psalm 51. Allow the water to drain and the candle to burn all the way down. This cleansing is good to do whenever you feel heavy at heart, guilty about having done something wrong, or as a preventative after doing some sort of left-handed work, an uncrossing or after handling cursed object.

Adam and Eve Candle Spell

Burn an Adam and Eve Lover's Candle to strengthen the passion and to bind your love with another. Write your petition with Dove's Blood ink on a piece of parch-ment paper and place under the candle. Dress the candle with a mixture of Fire of Love Oil and Adam and Eve Oil. Say the following prayer every day for seven days, or until the candle burns all the way down.

> *May the power of the symbolic love of Adam and Eve make me strong, attractive, and desirable so that I may enjoy your acts of love and kindness and make your joyful powers of love everlasting.*

Place the ritual remains in a brown paper bag and leave at a cross-roads.

Sweet Glove Gris Gris

Here is a gris gris spell attributed to the infamous Voodoo Queen, Marie Laveaux. If a woman is in love with a man who has not reciprocated her feelings, the woman is to get one of his gloves and fill it with honey and sugar to sweeten him up, and steel dust or magnetic sand to gain power over him. She should then tie the glove closed with red string and sleep with the glove under her mattress every night until her loved one comes to her. A slightly modernized modification of this gris gris is to use honey granules as opposed to honey in its sticky state.

Prevent a Man from Fraternizing

If you don't want your man to talk to another woman, take a nail and drive it at the end of his heel prints. He will run from her the next time he sees her.

Excerpted from *The Voodoo Hoodoo Spellbook* by Denise Alvarado.

Nasty Workings

by Madrina Angelique

Sometimes there are people who have done us very wrong, hurt us or someone we love and we feel the need for justice or revenge. While I don't condone going after everyone who steps on our toes, there are certainly times when nasty workings are justified. I always do a reading first to make sure the Spirits are willing to help. If I get an OK then I decide how I'm going to proceed and begin gathering my supplies.

I generally work in threes, meaning I will do three separate works for a single cause. I might do a jar spell with vinegar, black salt and goat milk paired with some work in the cemetery with darker Spirits and finish off with a piece of raw meat with the enemies name carved in it left to rot in the woods.

Protecting one's self, family, pets and property are a large part of Hoodoo and the ATR's. I always try to follow any negative working with a positive working to help keep the energies around me balanced. Keeping cleansed is also an important element in keeping energies balanced after negative workings. When beginning any negative work first make sure the work you are going to do is justified. Then decide how you want to proceed and write out your spell. Make a list of all ingredients you will need. I like to prepare a space for this kind of working somewhere out of the main stream of the house especially where children and pets can't get to it. A lot of times I will perform these kinds of works outside or off my property. I like to keep as much negative energy out of my space as possible. One thing to always remember is to not talk or brag about your workings, especially the negative ones. All that does is being in more negative energy toward you.

****

To Stop An Enemy

Take 9 cherimoya seeds and tie them into a black cloth along with your enemies photo. Tie the bundle with black thread. Take the bundle to the cemetery at midnight and bury it, cursing your enemy as you bury the bundle. This will poison the enemies life. A cherimoya is a fruit from central America. The fruit is edible but the seeds are highly toxic. They can be found in most Asian and international markets.

****

About the author: Madrina Angelique is initiated in the Palo and Santeria traditions. She is the author of *Workin' in da Boneyard* and *Crossroads Mamas 105 Spiritual Baths for Every Occasion,* and is a regular contributor to *Hoodoo and Conjure Magazine* and *Gumbo Ya Ya.*

Website: www.ritualwitch.com
FB Fan Page: https://www.facebook.com/madrinaangelique
Twitter: www.twitter.com/ritualwitch

SUPERSTITION, DEPRAVI

CORRECT PICTURE OF THE VOU-

To Ride A Horse:
The Possession Of The Lwa

by Melony Malsom

The Serpent And The Rainbow is a novel and movie that most of us with an interest in Voodoo have heard of or seen. The accounts, based on actual events, conjure up terrifying images of zombies, animal sacrifice, sacred rituals, and spirit possession. This kind of ritual possession must not be confused or integrated with the over marketed demonic possession of the cinema.

Spiritual possession in Voodoo is actually a wanted condition sought by the practitioner, worshipper, Mambo, or Houngan. The Lwa, usually one of particular significance to the rite performed, is chosen; invoked with the Lwa's vévé, a sacrifice (usually a chicken or goat), and ritual drumming and dancing by the participants. When the ritual reaches it's

ND LUST LOCKED ARMS.
CE DOWN TOWN ON TUESDAY !

height, a type of frenzy takes place in one or more of the seekers whereby they relinquish their bodies over to the Spirit. They have now become the horse and the Lwa their rider.

Horsing, as it is sometimes referred to, is a direct and very personal way for the practitioner or worshipper to be close to and become one with the Divine. They become a conduit of sorts for the Lwa's intense concentrated spiritual energy and will adopt the personality traits of that particular spirit. Depending on the situation and the Lwa chosen, some may become violent; tearing at their clothing, swearing, spitting, or even biting, as well as other physically violent acts causing the person being ridden to have to be restrained. Some Lwa, such Erzulie Freda, may adopt a kinder, gentler persona towards her followers. This mystifying phenomenon effects the person on a grand scale, spiritually, mentally, and physically, after which they are exhausted. Why do it at all? There are few experiences that can come close to becoming one with a Divine being. The worshipper usually comes away from the experience healed, able to heal, much wiser, or with a special message from the Lwa.

Spiritual possession by the Lwa is a sacred practice still utilized by devout Vodoun sects in Haitian, Caribbean, and Western civilizations. To become one with the Gods is as part of their religious practice as praying is to others. It is not evil or demonic. On the contrary, possession is a blessing and a sacred privilege. To be ridden by the lwa is an experience that transcends levels of consciousness that very few of us can only imagine.

****

About the author:
An artist and writer for over 20 years, Melony enjoys creating and selling encaustic pieces and her Evil Twin Conjure Products on Etsy. Melony is currently working on several writing and artistic endeavors, including an easy reference guide to the Lwa.

Facebook: www.facebook.com/melony.malsom

Random Conjure Quote

"The conjure-doctor has five distinct services to render to his patient. He must (i) tell him whether he is conjured or not, (2) he must find out who conjured him, (3) he must search for and find the 'trick' and destroy it, (4) he must cure the patient, (5) he will if the patient wishes turn back the trick upon the one who made it. A conjure-doctor summoned to attend a case of mysterious illness in a family will frequently begin his examination by putting a small piece of silver into the mouth or hand of the sufferer. Should the silver turn black, there is no doubt about the diagnosis."

The Journal of American Folklore, Vol. 9, No. 33 (Apr. - Jun., 1896) , pp. 143-147

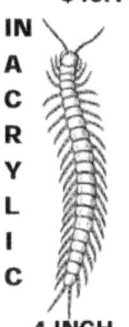

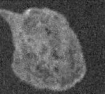

The
Goddesses
Of Antiquity

by
*Denise Alvarado and
Alyne Pustanio*

The Pearls of Aphrodite, by Herbert Draper.

Aphrodite

"Maker of the morning dew"

*A*phrodite is the Greek Goddess of love, beauty, pleasure, procreation and eternal youth. In addition, she is connected to the death and rebirth of nature and human beings. She is one of Twelve Olympians of the Greek pantheon, making her a major deity of worship. She is, in fact, considered the most attractive goddess of Mount Olympus, arousing desire to gods and humans, as well as birds and beasts. She is associated with the Roman goddess, Venus, and the Egyptian goddess, Hathor.

As with many Greek deities, there are several myths pertaining to Aphrodite's origin. According to Hesiod's *Theogony*, for example, she arose from the sea foam after Cronus castrated Uranus and threw his genitals into the sea. In another myth found in Homer's *Iliad*, she is the daughter of Zeus and Dione.

Aphrodite is said to have had many children and many lovers—both human men and gods. She was married to the lame smith Hephaestus, the Olympian God of Iron; however, it was Ares, God of War, to whom she was truly devoted and with whom she was having a passionate, but secret love affair.

According to myth, Aphrodite gave birth to Eros, the winged cupid of love and was often accompanied by him. Other children of Aphrodite were Himeros (sexual desire), Pothos (sexual desire), Phobos (fear), Deimos (terror), Armonia (Harmony) and the Nymph Rhode.

Modern Hellenistic Devotion to Aphrodite

Modern Hellenistic devotees of Aphrodite worship her as a Goddess of love and passion. She is petitioned for blessings in general, as well as specifically for help in the areas of relationships and sex. She is celebrated on three main festival days: 1) **Aphrodisia**, her primary day, celebrated with the Attic calendar on the 4th of *Hekatombaion* (between the months of July and August on the Gregorian calendar); 2) **Adonia**, a joint festival of Aphrodite and her partner Adonis, celebrated on the first full moon following the Northern spring equinox; and 3) on the

fourth of each month, which is considered a sacred day of both Aphrodite and her son Eros.[1]

Modern Pagan Devotion to Aphrodite

It is no surprise that Aphrodite is embraced in pagan circles where there are some commonly held beliefs and practices about her. Modern worship of Aphrodite within the context of Goddess worship is consistent with the Hellenistic worship in terms of conditions for which she is invoked. Honored as the Goddess of love and passion, Aphrodite is the go-to Goddess for matters regarding love, relationships and sex.

April is the month sacred to Aphrodite. It is the month of new beginnings, birth and renewal, and a time when we begin to see the first flowers of the year opening into full bloom. April's full moon is the Pink Moon. According to the Farmer's Almanac, April's Full Pink Moon is named after the herb moss pink, or wild ground phlox, which is one of the earliest widespread flowers of the spring. April is also associated with the wind, the element that gives us the energy and momentum we need to move forward. All of these energies in the month of April can be harnessed in invocations to Aphrodite.

Aphrodite's symbols include an apple, scallop shell and a mirror.[2] Her sacred animals include doves, sparrows, horses and swans. She is associated with a number of herbs, suggesting she may have been linked to herbal magic at one point in time. Some of the herbs attributed to her include apple, myrtle, poppy, rose, and water-mint. [3]

According to some pagan friends, an altar to Aphrodite should ideally have a statue or some sort of image of her on it. Keep a pink silk cloth or scarf that you can use to wrap her in. Some folks indicate her color is green and that two green candles should flank her statue. Rose quartz can be placed on her altar along with flowers and some of her other favorite things. Burn jasmine incense when invoking her as jasmine is considered to be her flower. Jasmine oil is her anointing oil, and everything on her altar including her statue as well as the devotee should be anointed with jasmine oil. I should note that in my research of her in examining the Greek myths and the Greek Magical Papyri, I have not seen jasmine specifically mentioned as associated with her. That's not to say it is not; it may be a modern pagan addition. Friday is her day of worship, with devotions beginning before sunrise when it is said she is most receptive.

To invoke the Goddess Aphrodite, anoint yourself and a pink candle with Aphrodite Oil (formulas are provided in the Goddess formulary). Make an offering to her. Offerings to Aphrodite can include honey cakes, incense, apples, figs, pomegranates and flowers. Then, say the following invocation take from *Sappho, The Hymn to Aphrodite* (1895), followed by your petition for your personal needs.

Immortal Aphrodite of the broidered throne, daughter of Zeus, weaver of wiles, I pray thee break not my spirit with anguish and distress, O Queen. But come hither, if ever before thou didst hear my voice afar, and listen, and leaving thy father's golden house camest with chariot yoked, and fair fleet sparrows drew thee, flapping fast their wings around the dark earth, from heaven through mid sky. Quickly arrived they; and thou, blessed one, smiling with immortal countenance, didst ask What now is befallen me, and Why now I call, and What I in my mad heart most desire to see. 'What Beauty now wouldst thou draw to love thee? Who wrongs thee, Sappho? For even if she flies she shall soon follow, and if she rejects gifts shall yet give, and if she loves not shall soon love, however loth.' Come, I pray thee, now too, and release me from cruel cares; and all that my heart desires to accomplish, accomplish thou, and be thyself my ally.[4]

Saucer Divination of Aphrodite

This spell is excerpted from *The Voodoo Doll Spellbook: A Compendium of Ancient and Contemporary Spells and Rituals*, the new version to be released June 2014 by Weiser Books. It is based on an actual spell described in the Greek Magical Papyri. For this spell, you will create a doll to represent the Greek goddess of love, Aphrodite. Use pink or red cloth for her body, and stuff her with cinnamon chips crushed well (or you can use powder, but you would have to use a lot more powder than small chips), rose petals, and marjoram. Marjoram was a favorite herb of the Greek goddess. It was said that if a girl put marjoram on her bed, Aphrodite would visit her and reveal her future spouse. Once you create your doll, set her on your altar. Right before bedtime, follow the directions of the Ancients from Greek Magickal Papyri provided below.
[5]

Having kept oneself Pure for 7 days, take a White Saucer, fill It with Water and Olive Oil, having previously written on Its Base with Myrrh Ink: "E'IOCH CHIPHA ELAMPSE'R ZE'L A E E' I O Y O"' (25 letters [in Greek]); and beneath the Base, on the outside: "TACHIE'L CNTHONIE' DRAXO'" (18 letters). Wax over with White Wax. On the outside of the Rim at the Top: "IERMI PHILO' 6 ERIKO'MA DERKO' MALO'K GAULE' APHRIE'L I ask" (say it 3 times). Let It rest on the Floor and looking intently at It, say "I call upon You, the Mother and Mistress of Nymphs, ILAOCH OBRIE' LOUCH TLOR; Come in, Holy Light, and give Answer, showing Your Lovely Shape!"
Then look intently at the Bowl. When you see Her, welcome Her and say, "Hail, Very Glorious Goddess, ILARA OUCH. And if You give me a Response, ex- tend Your Hand." And when She extends It, expect Answers

to your Inquiry.

But if She does not listen, say, "I call upon the ILAOUCH who has begotten Himeros, the Lovely Horai and You Graces; I also call upon the Zeus-sprung Physis [Nature] of All ings, two-formed, indivisible, straight, foam-beau- tiful Aphrodite. Reveal to me Your Lovely Light and Your Lovely Face, O Mistress ILAOUCH. I conjure You, Giver of Fire, by ELGINAL, and by the Great Names OBRIE'TYCH KERDYNOUCHILE'PSIN NIOU NAUNIN IOUTHOU THRIGX TATIOUTH GERTIATH GERGERIS GERGERIE' THEITHI. I also ask You by the All Wonderful Names, OISIA EI EI AO' E'Y AAO' IO'IAIAIO' SO'THOU BERBROI AKTEROBORE GERIE' IE'OYA; bring me Light and Your Lovely Face and the True Saucer Divination, You shining with Fire, bearing Fire all around, stirring the Land from afar, IO' IO' PHTHAIE' THOUTHOI PHAEPHI. Do it!"

Preparation: having kept yourself Pure, as you learned, take a Bronze Drinking Cup, and write with Myrrh Ink the previously inscribed Stele [charm or amulet] which calls upon Aphrodite, and use the untouched Olive Oil and clean River Water. Put the Drinking Cup on your Knees and speak over it the Stele mentioned above, and the Goddess will appear to you and will reveal concerning what Things you wish.[6]

The Myth of Aphrodite, Paris and the Golden Apple

According to one version in Greek mythology, the following myth is the origin of the infamous Trojan War, which lasted for ten years.

It all started when Eris, the goddess of discord, realized that she had not been invited to the marriage of the King Peleus with the sea Nymph Thetis- a marriage that took place on the Mountain of Pelion in Thessaly, in Central Greece. Eris was so furious about her exclusion that she decided to go to the wedding and throw a golden apple, the fruit of temptation, to the banquet table. The apple was supposed to go out to the "Calliste"- the fairest one. Three goddesses claimed the beautiful golden apple: Hera, the mature goddess of Marriage, Athena, the sophisticated goddess of Wisdom and Aphrodite, the sensual goddess of Love.

Zeus, the King of the gods, had a hard time deciding, since all three were dear to him, so he left the judgment to the most handsome young man—the Trojan Prince Paris.

Hera and Athena did their best to bribe Paris with power and glory, while Aphrodite seduced him with love and the most beautiful woman in the world: the legendary Helen of Sparta.

Paris opted for Aphrodite and so Helen was taken away from Sparta to become Helen of Troy.[7]

QUICK FACTS

Greek name: Aphrodite
Roman Name: Venus
Egyptian Association: Hathor
Patronage: Love, beauty, the arts, fertility, sexual rapture, sailors
Day: Friday
Months: April
Greek Holy Day: Aphrodisiac Festival
Symbols: scepter, myrtle, dove
Candle Color: pink and red
Planetary Association: Venus
Herbs, Plants & Foods: Cinnamon, apple, cypress, marjoram, myrtle, olive, orris, pomegranates, lime trees
Flowers: Rose, daisy, iris
Mineral: Abalone
Animals: sea, dolphins, doves, swans, clams, scallop shells and pearls

The Birth of Venus by Sandro Botticelli, *circa* 1485

Artemis

"Artemis of the wildland, Mistress of Animals"

One of the most popular Goddesses in Greece, Artemis is the Greek goddess of the hunt, the moon and protector of pregnant women and the children. She is the daughter of Zeus and Leto and is Apollo's twin sister. Like other Greek deities, she was bringer of both blessings and curses. Her patronage includes protection of young girls, wild animals, wilderness, childbirth, and virginity. She is identified with the Roman Goddess Diana and the Egyptian Goddess Bastet.

Although Artemis was worshipped throughout Greece, she was especially venerated in Arcadia. She lived in the wild, untamed forests there and was considered the most pure of all the Goddesses. As a virgin, "Artemis had interested many gods and men, but only her hunting companion, Orion, won her heart."[6] According to myth, "Orion foolishly boasted that he would slay all the beasts of the earth. Gaia (the Earth) sent forth a scorpion to slay him, and when he fell, the grief-stricken Artemis placed him amongst the stars as the constellation Orion."[8]

In classical Greek mythology, Artemis is often depicted with a bow and arrow, flanked by two lions, or in ecstatic dance with a stag. Later she is shown standing on a lion; finally, she stands with her bow, holding a slain deer in each hand.

Artemis' attributes include a bow and arrow, apparently so that she can bring death and disease to young women. Gold chariots, spears, nets, and a lyre are also among her symbols. Animals sacred to her include deer, bears, hunting dogs, boars, guinea fowls and buzzard hawks. Plants sacred to Artemis include palms, amaranth, cypress, cedar and asphodel. Asphodel flowers were abundant in the **Asphodel Meadows**, which was a place in the Ancient Greek underworld where ordinary souls go to live after death.[9] The medicinal herb *Artemisia*, commonly called Mugwort, is named after her and is among her sacred herbs, as well.

Favors from Artemis included blessings in hunting, fishing, good health, recovery from illness and successful childbirth and survival of

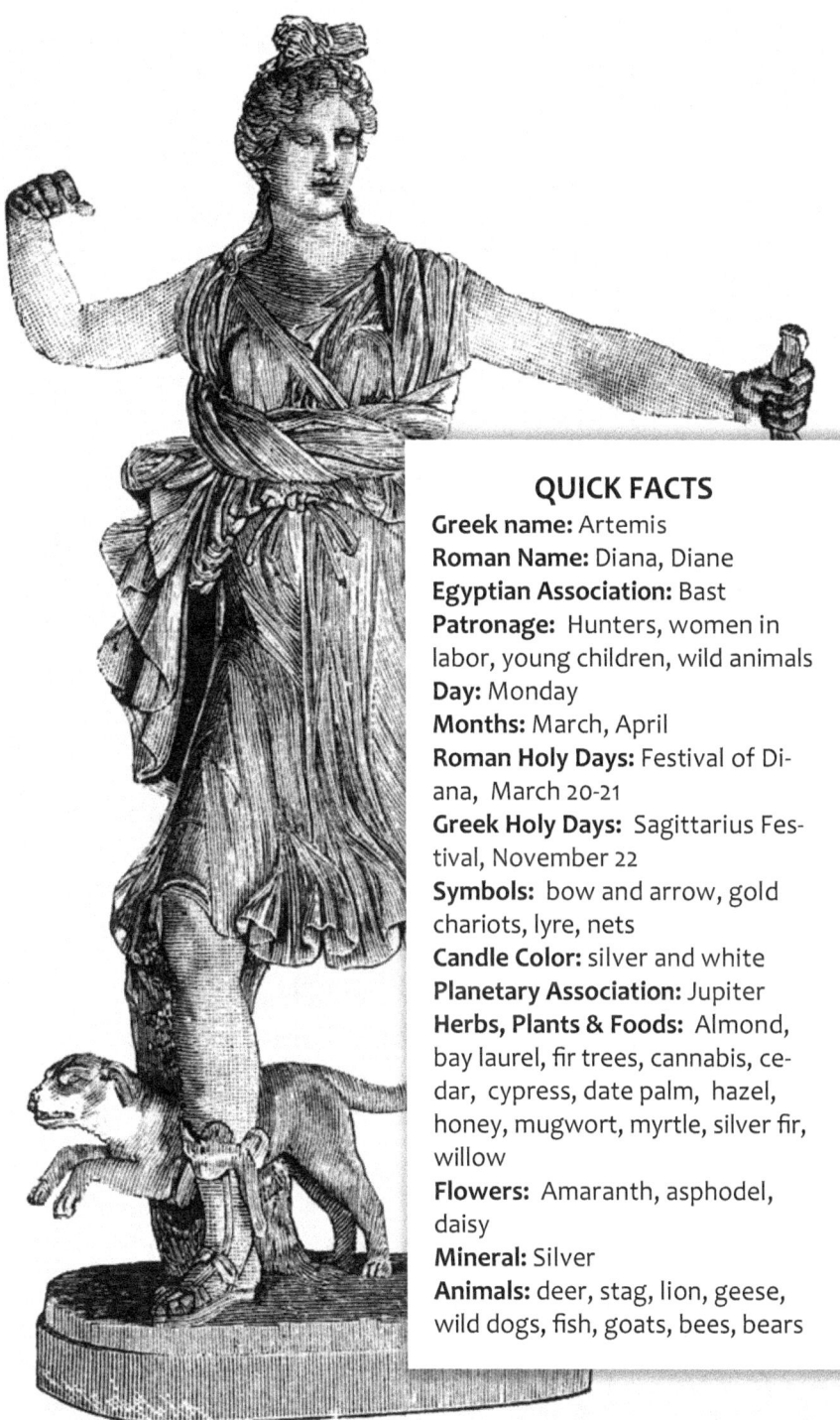

QUICK FACTS

Greek name: Artemis
Roman Name: Diana, Diane
Egyptian Association: Bast
Patronage: Hunters, women in labor, young children, wild animals
Day: Monday
Months: March, April
Roman Holy Days: Festival of Diana, March 20-21
Greek Holy Days: Sagittarius Festival, November 22
Symbols: bow and arrow, gold chariots, lyre, nets
Candle Color: silver and white
Planetary Association: Jupiter
Herbs, Plants & Foods: Almond, bay laurel, fir trees, cannabis, cedar, cypress, date palm, hazel, honey, mugwort, myrtle, silver fir, willow
Flowers: Amaranth, asphodel, daisy
Mineral: Silver
Animals: deer, stag, lion, geese, wild dogs, fish, goats, bees, bears

Artemis, from Manual of Mythology, 1895, public domain.

newborns. Her curses included illness, disease, sudden death, death in childbirth, stillborn infants, stunted growth, plagues, animals sent to plague humans and hunting injuries.

Modern Worship of Artemis

Artemis is among the Goddesses that are worshipped by modern pagans. Invocations of Artemis should ideally be done outside. Cast a circle using barley water around you and anoint yourself and a green or brown candle with Artemis Oil (formula provided in the Goddess formulary). Place some of her symbols around the candle. Burn some storax incense and recite the following (translated) Greek hymn to Artemis, followed by your personal petition.

To Prothyraia [Artemis], Fumigation from Storax. O venerable Goddess, hear my prayer, for labour pains are thy peculiar care. In thee, when stretched upon the bed of grief, the sex, as in a mirror, view relief. Guard of the race, endued with gentle mind, to helpless youth benevolent and kind; benignant nourisher; great nature's key belongs to no divinity but thee. Thou dwellest with all immanifest to sight, and solemn festivals are thy delight. Thine is the task to loose the virgin's zone and thou in every work art seen and known. With births you sympathise, though pleased to see the numerous offspring of fertility. When racked with labour pangs, and sore distressed the sex invoke thee, as the soul's sure rest; for thou Eileithyia alone canst give relief to pain, which art attempts to ease, but tries in vain. Artemis Eileithyia, venerable power, who bringest relief in labour's dreadful hour; hear, Prothyraia and make the infant race thy constant care.[10]

THE MYTHS OF ARTEMIS
Apollo and the Tears of Niobe: A Punishment Story

"Niobe was the wife of Amphion, the King of Thebes. Together they had seven sons and seven daughters. Niobe and Amphion were very proud of their children.

Until day, Niobe started boasting that she was superior than Leto, since Leto was only blessed with two children,Apollo, the god of the sun and Artemis, the goddess of the hunt. Outraged by the insult, Leto swore revenge on Niobe, so she asked from her children Apollo and Artemis to eliminate Niobe's children one by one.

Apollo and Artemis obeyed and they killed all fourteen children with arrows dipped in poison. Apollo aimed at the male, whereas Artemis aimed at the female children. After their awful death, Niobe's children had to remain without burial for nine whole days, because Zeus, the

King of the Gods, promised he would turn anyone who attempted to bury the children into stone.

The royal couple was inconsolable. Amphion committed suicide, while Niobe resorted to Sipylos, a city of the Near East. Once there, she pleaded with the gods for mercy, asking them to take away her life. The gods finally sympathized and they turned Niobe into stone, placing her at the peak of the city.

Ever since that day, every summer, one can see drops of water seeping out of the stone's pores...they are nothing but the tears of Niobe!"[11]

Artemis and Actaeon: A Punishment Story

One day, while Actaeon was on his way to hunt, he stumbled upon the divine virgin Artemis, bathing naked in the woods of Orchomenos, surrounded by her Nymphs. He was so entranced by her beautiful body and divine grace, that he couldn't help but stare.

When Artemis became aware of this intrusion, she got furious and punished Actaeon by transforming him into a stag.

Actaeon became fearful and fled away, but his own hunting dogs, 50 in number, jumped on him and tore him to pieces and devoured him, thinking that he was a real stag. [12]

Athena

"There they made her a soldier"

 $\mathcal{A}$ thena, the Grey-Eyed and the Ægis-bearer, is the goddess of wisdom, crafts and war. She is the virgin patroness of Athens, originally a Creten Goddess who watched over the home and town. She is known as the daughter of Zeus, born without a mother. According to the most common origin myth, she was born fully armored from the Zeus' forehead with a war cry. She is likened to the Roman Goddess Minerva and the Egyptian deity Neith.

While Athena is called a goddess of war, she did not like war and preferred to use wisdom to settle disputes. Thus, a more correct description of this patronage would be patron of war strategy. She was cunning, disciplined and strategic when it came to battle. There is no better example of this than her participation in the infamous Trojan War. She was the brainchild behind the device of the Trojan Horse built by Odysseus and Epeios.

Athena was revered throughout Greece where there were numerous shrines and temples to her. Sacrifices offered to Athena included female bulls, rams and cows. No female lambs were offered to her. Human sacrifices of maidens and boys were made once a year in Ilion as atonement for the crime committed by the Locrian Ajax upon Cassandra.[13]

As goddess of arts and crafts, Athena favored weaving. According to myth: "Long before there were palaces, the Goddess appeared to a group of women gathering plants in a field. She broke open the stems of the blue-flowered flox and showed them how the threadlike fibers could be spun and then woven. The woof and warp danced in her fingers until a length of cloth was born before their eyes. She told them which plants and roots would color the cloth, and then she led them to a pit of clay. There they watched Athena form and smooth vessels, statues, and trinkets which she covered with symbols of ever-repeating circles that were kept by women for centuries."[14]

Athena's attributes include Aegis, spear, pomegranate, owl, distaff, and helmet. Her patronage includes Animals sacred to her include the serpent - a symbol of perpetual renewal, owl, cock and crow. The olive

QUICK FACTS

Greek name: Athena
Roman Name: Minerva
Egyptian Association: Neith
Patronage: Wisdom, war, arts and crafts, spiritual quests, courage, architects, inspiration, civilization, law and justice, just warfare, mathematics, strength, strategy, skill, lesbians
Months: June, July
Symbols: spear, aegis, distaff, helmet
Candle Color: purple and white
Planetary Association: Mars
Herbs, Plants & Foods: apple, olive, pomegranate
Flowers: flox, blue flowers
Animals: owl , serpent, cock, crow

Drawing of Athena Parthenos, artist   unknown. From Harper's Weekly, August 6, 1892, p.d.

tree and olive oil were also sacred to her.

Modern Worship of Athena

Athena is still worshipped by some folks in Greece, a testament to her importance in the Greek pantheon. Make an altar for Athena of olive branches, blue flowers, figurines of serpents, a statue or image of her, and a blue candle. Give offerings of fruit and cake. Anoint yourself and the candle with Athena Ritual Oil (formula provided in the Goddess formulary) and make your petition.

Hymn to Athena

[1] Of Pallas Athena, guardian of the city, I begin to sing. Dread is she, and with Ares she loves deeds of war, the sack of cities and the shouting and the battle. It is she who saves the people as they go out to war and come back.

[5] Hail, goddess, and give us good fortune with happiness![15]

Myth of Athena

This myth concerns the contest with Poseidon for dominion of Athens in which she produced the first olive tree and he the first horse.

"Kekrops, a son of the soil, with a body compounded of man and serpent, was the first king of Attika . . . In his time, they say, the gods resolved to take possession of cities in which each of them should receive his own peculiar worship. So Poseidon was the first that came to Attika, and with a blow of his trident on the middle of the acropolis, he produced a sea which they now call Erekhtheis. After him came Athena, and, having called on Kekrops to witness her act of taking possession, she planted an olive tree, which is still shown in the Pandrosion. But when the two strove for possession of the country, Zeus parted them and appointed arbiters, not, as some have affirmed, Kekrops and Kranaus, nor yet Erysikhthon, but the twelve gods (*dodekatheoi*). And in accordance with their verdict the country was adjudged to Athena, because Kekrops bore witness that she had been the first to plant the olive. Athena, therefore, called the city Athens after herself, and Poseidon in hot anger flooded the Thriasian plain and laid Attika under the sea."[16]

Hecate

"She who devours the light"

Hecate – sometimes called Hekate or Heket – was born of the fecund and primordial Dark Mother of the Abyss, the Cthonic night goddess Nyx. A Titan Goddess of the Greek pantheon who, as a help-meet to Zeus aided in his defeat of the Gigante, Hecate was absorbed into the Olympic myths and legends and allowed to keep her Titanic status. Yet, her nature was so threatening that the ancient Greeks were constantly bewildered over how to classify her; they found it necessary to diffuse her primal, dark feminine power by mixing her into other legends. Over time Hecate became increasingly marginalized until at last she was transformed into a lesser goddess, tasked with illuminating the paths of the Underworld with the light of her torches and guiding lost souls to and from the subterranean realm.

In this latter manifestation, Hecate the Mighty One became the guide of Persephone after her abduction by Hades to the Underworld. Persephone was, in fact, a later goddess who resulted from a watered-down image of Hecate's own dark divinity. It is Hecate, bearing the single light in the impenetrable darkness of Hades, who leads Persephone to reunion each spring with her mother Demeter. It is Hecate who meets Persephone when her time with Demeter is over, leading her back into the bowels of Hell. Relegated to the serviceable position of gatekeeper, Hecate was portrayed as a moon goddess adorned with a crown of stars and bearing a torch that burns eternally. In this tame manifestation Hecate entered the Eleusinian rites of birth, death and rebirth that marked the cycles of nature.

Over the generations, witches who honored and served Hecate came to know very well that this particular portion of her mythology was simply the result of ancient Greeks confronted with something the primal female power of which they could not grasp and so, perhaps unintentionally, they minimized her role in their pantheon in order to better understand her. In fact, it was the scholars and Inquisitors of the medieval Church who hit nearest the mark in understanding this personification of the imposing Crone Goddess, Queen of the year's darkest months, although they easily fell prey to their own fears and prejudices, hanging upon her the Ugly Hag aspect that would persist through centuries of misunderstanding. Thus, Hecate took the blame for enticing Christians away from the path of God and into the hands of Satan, aiding pagans and heathens in their dark rites and devil worship – again, a subtle denouement, an attempt to lessen her singular, feminine power by portraying her in service to God's Enemy, Satan.

She was known by many names, this pagan goddess of death and darkness: Nocticula, Invincible Queen of Night, Mother of Witches, Mistress of Magic; Foul Queen of Corpses, Guardian of the Crossroads; as Queen of the Dead she was known as Prytania; as night-raider from Hell she was called Agriope, the Savage Faced. A cosmic being, she was one of the most ancient manifestations of the All Powerful Triple Goddess; her very name meant "eater of light" and she was the Goddess most often associated with magick, divination, the underworld and burial grounds, death and the secrets kept by the dead. A guardian of crossroads and other in-between places she was associated with commanding the passages between this world and the world of the unseen; she allows souls to travel to and from the spirit world and escorts souls of the newly-dead to their home on the other side; thus, she is associated with burying grounds and cemeteries. Her aspect as a fertility goddess is highly sexualized and lust and licentiousness are said to flow from Hecate's influence; similarly, she haunts the dreams of men and communicates prophecies to humankind in the symbols of our dreams.

Wild animals are sacred to Hecate and she is sometimes depicted with three animal heads – dog, horse and bear, but her primary animal familiar is the black dog. Her approach at the borders of our world is heralded by the wild howling and baying of her hell hounds, packs of huge black dogs that accompany her and draw her chariot – constructed of human bones – into the world of the unsuspecting living. Hecate also brought huge cats with her, foul beasts of Hades that prowled and snatched in silence as victims of the hounds fell before them. Sometimes she appeared in the three-headed form by which many worshipped her; other times she was seen as an unbearable beautiful female, naked, with a head full of black and flowing hair and eyes that burned with balefire light. Other times, she delighted in appearing as the hag, with a face that could strike terror to the heart or bring instant death to the unwary or unprepared.

Behind her, in her wake, was her army of the Dead – pale, skeletal wraiths in various stages of decomposition and death. Her Captains rode upon lean black horses and her legions followed behind, a writhing, gibbering mass that smelled of a thousand open graves. And, Hec-

QUICK FACTS
Greek name: Hecate
Patronage: Crossroads, underworld, death, corpses, ghosts, magic, witches, witchcraft, divination, liminality, dreams, prophecy, fertility, maiden, mother, crone
Feast Day: November 16
Symbols: torch, black dog
Candle Color: red and green
Planetary Association: Moon
Herbs, Plants & Foods: yew, black poplar, willow
Animals: dogs, horses, bears, wild animals, black dog

Hecate, Greek Goddess of the crossroads; drawing by Stephanie Mallarmé in *Les Dieux Antiques, nouvelle mythologie illustrée* in Paris, 1880, p.d.

ate was a storm bringer whose coming in ancient times has been blamed for deluges and floods that claimed thousands of lives.

Witches seek Hecate at crossroads and in ancient groves or empty fields, desolate and open to the night sky. In her aspect as Queen of Witches, Hecate sometimes crosses over less furiously, choosing instead to walk the roads and byways on All Hallows' Eve as a mature woman, clad in black, carrying a torch to light her way and accompanied by a large black dog. She is often found awaiting witches under the spreading branches of a black poplar or willow tree, although the yew tree – which is said to root in the mouths of the dead – is the tree most associated with this Crone of Death.

In her aspect as Goddess of death and the cycle of rebirth, it is said by witches that Hecate is the Goddess to call upon when you seek to honor the end of a cycle in your life or when you wish to lose something of yourself.

Hecate is venerated and worshipped in the dark hours of her feast, November 16th.[17]

Orphic Hymn 1 to Hecate

"Hekate Einodia, Trioditis [Trivia], lovely dame, of earthly, watery, and celestial frame, sepulchral, in a saffron veil arrayed, pleased with dark ghosts that wander through the shade; Perseis, solitary goddess, hail! The world's key-bearer, never doomed to fail; in stags rejoicing, huntress, nightly seen, and drawn by bulls, unconquerable queen; Leader, Nymphe, nurse, on mountains wandering, hear the suppliants who with holy rites thy power revere, and to the herdsman with a favouring mind draw near." [18]

Egyptian Charm to Dissolve a Spell

This spell is taken from an ancient Egyptian papyrus text (circa 3rd or 4th century A.D.) and offers protection against Hekate, a Greek goddess who haunted crossroads and frightened passers-by.

"Askei kataski erôn oreôn iôr mega semnuêr bauï," (three times), "Phobantia, remember, I have been initiated, and I went down into the chamber of the Dactyls, and I saw the other things down below, virgin, dog," etc. Say it at the crossroads, and turn around and flee, because it is at those places that she appears. Say it late at night, about what you wish, and it will reveal it in your sleep; and if you are led away to death, say these things while scattering seeds of sesame, and it will save you.[19]

References

1. Aphrodite - Wikipedia, the free encyclopedia. (n.d.). Retrieved from http://en.wikipedia.org/wiki/Greek_goddess_of_love
2. Retrieved from http://www.theoi.com/Olympios/Aphrodite.html
3. Heckart, K. (n.d.). *Pre-Hellenic Goddesses*. Retrieved from http://www.kelleyheckart.com/Pre-Hellenic_Goddesses.html
4. Wharton, H. T. (1895). *Sappho, The Hymn to Aphrodite*, 3rd edition, London: John Lane.
5. Alvarado, D. (2014). *The Voodoo Doll Spellbook: A Compendium of Ancient and Contemporary Spells and Rituals.* Red Wheel/Weiser.
6. *The Greek Magical Papyri in Translation, Including the Demotic Spells, Volume 1,* Hans Dieter Betz, Ed. (Chicago: University of Chicago Press).
7. Hatzitsinidou, E. (2013). *Aphrodite, the Greek Goddess of Love, Pleasure and Beauty.* Retrieved from: http://www.greek-gods.info/greek-gods/aphrodite/myths/aphrodite-paris-golden-apple/
8. *What is the story of the Goddess Artemis?* | ChaCha. (n.d.). Retrieved from http://www.chacha.com/question/what-is-the-story-of-the-goddess-artemis
9. *Asphodel Meadows* - Wikipedia, the free encyclopedia. (n.d.). Retrieved from http://en.wikipedia.org/wiki/Asphodel_Meadows
10. The Hymns of Orpheus: Translated from the Original Greek With a Preliminary Dissertation on the Life and Theology of Orpheus to Which Is Added the E. Translation by Taylor, Thomas (1792). University of Pennsylvania Press, 1999. London: Bertram Dobell.
11. Hatzitsinidou, E. (2013). Artemis, Goddess of the Hunt and the Moon Retrieved from: http://www.greek-gods.info/greek-gods/artemis/myths/tears-of-niobe/
12. Greek Stories about Artemis-Artemis and Actaeon. (n.d.). Retrieved from http://www.greek-gods.info/greek-gods/artemis/myths/artemis-actaeon/
13. ATHENA : Greek Goddess of Wisdom, Crafts & War | Mythology ... (n.d.). Retrieved from http://www.theoi.com/Olympios/Athena.html
14. Athena - Wikipedia, the free encyclopedia. (n.d.). Retrieved from http://en.wikipedia.org/wiki/Athena
15. Homeric Hymn 11 to Athena (trans. Evelyn-White) (Greek epic C7th to 4th B.C.)
16. Pseudo-Apollodorus, Bibliotheca 3. 14. 1 (trans. Frazer) (Greek mythographer C2nd A.D.)
17. Hecate article reprinted from Alvarado, D., Dean, C., Pustanio, A. (2012). *Hoodoo Almanac 2012,* Prescott Valley, AZ: Creole Moon Publications.

18. Orphic Hymn 1 to Hecate
19. http://www.lib.umich.edu/traditions-magic-late-antiquity/ rb.display.html

Athenian tetradrachm representing the goddess Athena. Image by Lequenne Gwendoline, licensed under the Creative Commons Attribution-Share Alike 3.0 Unported license. http://en.wikipedia.org/wiki/Athena

Formulas & Recipes of the Goddesses

by Denise Alvarado

Aphrodite Ritual Oil

The Greek Goddess of love is associated with the herbs and oils that comprise this formula. This oil is said to protect wandering wives from discovery by their husbands and to increase sexual attraction. Can be used to influence a platonic relationship to move to a more intimate one. Combine rose, pomegranate and mint with a pinch of poppy seeds in a base of olive oil. Use to anoint red candles or wear as a perfume.

Aphrodite Perfume Oil

Another formula for Aphrodite Oil is mostly jasmine. Combine jasmine essential oil with a hint of rose and add a few jasmine buds in the oil. Use to anoint her altar and items ion her altar. Devotees can wear this perfume oil when invoking and making offerings to her.

Aphrodite's Greek Honey Cakes
Ingredients

- 1 cup all-purpose flour
- 1 1/2 teaspoons baking powder
- 1/4 teaspoon salt
- 1/2 teaspoon ground cinnamon
- 1 teaspoon orange zest
- 3/4 cup butter
- 3/4 cup white sugar
- 3 eggs
- 1/4 cup milk
- 1 cup chopped walnuts
- 1 cup white sugar1 cup honey
- 3/4 cup water1 teaspoon lemon juice

Directions

1. Preheat oven to 350 degrees F (175 degrees C). Grease and flour a 9 inch square pan. Combine the flour, baking powder, salt, cinnamon and orange rind. Set aside.
2. In a large bowl, cream together the butter and 3/4 cup sugar until light and fluffy. Beat in the eggs one at a time. Beat in the flour mixture alternately with the milk, mixing just until incorporated. Stir in the walnuts.
3. Pour batter into prepared pan. Bake in the preheated oven for 40 minutes, or until a toothpick inserted into the center of the cake comes out clean. Allow to cool for 15 minutes, then cut into diamond shapes. Pour honey syrup over the cake.
4. For the Honey Syrup: In a saucepan, combine honey, 1 cup sugar and water. Bring to a simmer and cook 5 minutes. Stir in lemon juice, bring to a boil and cook for 2 minutes.
(Allrecipes.com http://allrecipes.com/recipe/greek-honey-cake)

Artemis Ritual Oil

Goddess of the hunt, wilderness and wild animals, this conjure oil is made with herbs sacred to her. Use both essential oils and herbs to make this oil. Combine mugwort, cypress and oak moss in a base of pure olive oil. Use to anoint green or brown candles or wear as a perfume.

Astarte Ritual Oil

Astarte is the Greek Goddess of sexuality, fertility and war. Astarte is the Greek name of the Mesopotamian Semitic goddess Ishtar. One of her symbols, the star within a circle, indicates she is associated with the planet Venus and has been deified as the evening star. This formula uses ingredients traditionally used as offerings to her in Greek mythology. Combine frangipani, honey and a pinch of ashes to a base of olive oil. Use to attract new opportunities for love and to enhance lovemaking. Use to anoint red or pink candles, with the planetary Seal of Venus, or wear as a perfume oil.

Athena Ritual Oil

The Greek virginal goddess of wisdom, art and war, the olive tree and the serpent were sacred to her. Thus, the formula for her oil is pure olive oil with a pinch of olive leaves and snake sheds.

Diana Ritual Oil

Often considered the Roman equivalent of Artemis, Diana is the goddess of the hunt, woods and the moon. Like Artemis, she is associated wild animals is said to have the power to communicate with and control animals. In Stregheria, she is embraced as the Queen of the Witches.

To make her anointing oil, blend orris root, oak moss, musk, and night jasmine with olive oil. Add a bit of dried oak leaf. Use to anoint green or brown candles or wear as a perfume.

Fortuna Ritual Oil

Fortuna was the Roman goddess of luck, fortune and fate; thus, she is invoked for wealth, abundance, good luck and prosperity. She is also a favorite among gamblers. Fortuna oil is ideal for anointing charms and seals associated with luck and money, yellow, orange and green candles, and altar items. It can also be worn as a perfume oil.

To make Fortuna Oil, combine oak bark with bay laurel, cloves, sweet orange, almond and olive oil as a base. Add some 18 carat gold flakes to the bottle.

Gaia's Honey and Barley Cakes

Gaia is the ancient Earth Mother who is responsible for giving birth to the human race. Traditionally, honey and barley cakes were offered to Gaia prior to collecting plants and herbs for healing. These cakes were favored among shepherds and travelers because they kept well and were a good alternative to fresh bread when it wasn't available. The secret to capturing the ancient tasty flavor is to toast the cakes after baking. Here's the recipe for Gaia's honey and barley cakes.

Ingredients
- 2 cups pearl barley
- 2 cups buttermilk
- 3/4/cup water
- 2 cups barley flour
- 1 teaspoon flour

Directions
Soak the pearl barley in buttermilk overnight. Preheat oven to 350 degrees. Line a square baking dish with baker's parchment, or rub with oil and dust with flour to prevent sticking. Place the soaked barley mixture in a food processor and add the water. Pulse and add the barley flour and salt until well mixed. Pour into prepared pan and bake for 30 to 40 minutes until firm but not completely dry.

Turn out the cake from the pan and allow to cool. Cut into 1 inch slices and toast in the oven at 325 degrees for 10 minutes each side, or

FOR:TVNA.

Engraving of *Fortuna*, 1541 by Hans Sebold Beham, p.d.

until dried out (Kaufman, 2006).

Hecate Ritual Oil
This is a powerful ritual oil of the goddess of the crossroads, magic and witchcraft. Combine thyme, mint, lavender, willow, yew, a pinch of crossroads dirt from a three way crossroads and a moonstone to a base of almond oil. Anoint ritual tools and self when invoking her.

Isis Ritual Oil
Isis is the Egyptian Mother Goddess of nature and magic, and patron of the Dead and children. She is often invoked for protection and healing. Combine myrrh, rose, and lotus to a base of corn oil and use to anoint green candles.

Persephone Ritual Oil
Persephone is the Greek Goddess of the Underworld, harvest, vegetation and spring growth. She is invoked for regeneration and agrarian magic. Persephone can also be invoked to bestow curses upon men who rape and abduct women and children. Her ritual oil consists of lavender, Lily of the Valley, and vanilla in a base of almond oil. Use to anoint black candles and invoke her for spirit communication and seership. Another formula for Persephone Oil combines apple, honey, fig, melon and pomegranate to a base of corn oil. Use with green and yellow candles. For cursing, add a pinch of ashes and earth collected during the dead of winter or graveyard dirt to the oil and use with brown and black candles.

Venus Perfume Oil
Venus is the popular Roman Goddess of love, sex, beauty, fertility, charm, seduction and prosperity. A most popular Goddess of romantic love, Venus oil is said to make the one who wears it irresistible to the opposite sex. Combine rose, myrtle, and mint to a base of grapeseed oil and wear as a perfume oil or use to anoint red and pink candles.

Vesta Ritual Oil and Powder
In Roman mythology, Vesta is the goddess of hearth, home and family. To make Vesta Oil, combine lotus Ad a pinch of salt and oak bark. Use for blessing the home, ridding the home of evil, and preparing a space for ritual use. It can also be used as an anointing oil to assist in gaining clarity, focus and concentration about a specific issue or in general.

As Vesta is associated with fire, a flash powder can be made for her. I do not recommend it to be used as a sprinkle throughout the home or anywhere else. Combine sulphur, charcoal and saltpeter and add to any herbal incense blend to make it self-lighting. Pour a small amount in a fire-proof dish and light it while invoking her. The flames will function to purify a space making it sacred and ready for ritual use.

References

Kaufman, C.K. (2006). *Cooking in Ancient Civilizations*, Westport CT: Greenwood Press.

Cross-Cultural Symbols of Protection

Symbols for protection from many cultures can be drawn and put into mojo bags, placed under candles or inscribed on candles for ritual protection work.

Helm of Awe (ægishjálmr) - magical symbol and warrior shield worn by Vikings for invincibility. Modern day use by Ásatrú followers for protection.

Buddhist parasol used for protection against the elements, suffering and evil influences.

Egyptian Eye of Horus for protection.

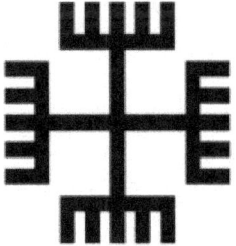

Hands of God, Slavic Neopaganism.

Saints of the Greater East End

by Oskar "Doc Mojo" Yetzirah

Moving back to the Greater East End has been a lot of fun. It is a different world here, and there are two ways of arriving. You get here by already knowing how, or, by getting lost in Downtown Houston. Texas Street feeds you right into one of the main veins of the Greater East End—Harrisburg. The Greater East End has been the home to Latinos in Houston since the late 1960s. Settled by Second and Third generations of Latino Americanos moving to Houston from South Texas, looking for a better life. Our Ancestors brought with them Tacos and Tamales; Raspas and Aquas. They brought with them, Los Santos.

The Saints play a great role here in the Greater East End, but not like they do on the South West Side of Houston. There, the Santos take the role of Orishas and are summoned by the beat of the drum and the calls of the Baba. Here, Los Santos are summoned by the soft whispers of our Grandmothers over a Rosary, and the heartfelt pleas of the working class before leaving the house.

Los Fieles ("the Faithful"), as they are called by the Cristianos, ask you, "What is the day of your Saint?" instead of "When is your birthday?" The faithful may have a small pewter pendant around their neck of the saint their mother may have prayed to during pregnancy and while giving birth. The Faithful may hold the Rosary as a sacred item that wards away El Diablo and keeps you safe from evil spirits and Mal Ojo. The Faithful may not always go to mass on Sunday, but will have an altar in their homes that they cross themselves in front of daily. The Faithful walk past an image of a Saint or of El Cristo and grace themselves three times.

Among Los Fieles, you will find La Doña, or Señora, the older lady who fixes candles and prepares charms. Unlike Botánicas where you can buy an already prepared candle, La Señora tells you, "Bring me a candle of Saint Martha, Green. Bring with you the Oil of Saint Martha. Bring me cloves and Hyssop."

When you return with these items, La Señora will dress the candle with the oil and speak prayers over it. In un molcajete, she will grind the cloves and hyssop together praying to Saint Martha, asking her to bless you in your need. She will tie ribbons around the top of the candle and kiss them as if they were the very robes of the Saint herself.

Lifting the completed candle, she will put it to your forehead and with it, make the sign of the cross on you, saying, "Saint Martha, bless this child." Putting the candle in your hands, she will reach over and whisper in your ear a blessing.

Growing up, my grandmother was this Señora. Until about two years ago, it was still common to see a young lady coming out of my grandmother's house with a candle in their hand.

Here in the Greater East End, I love seeing that this tradition is still alive and strong—and I know that it will never die. There are within the barrios a common thread of saints who are kept very well in stock in the grocery stores here. Santa Barbara, Santa Marta, San Martín Caballero, San Judas Tadeo and San Francisco de Assisi.

Santa Marta is the patron saint of the bus boys, waiters, mariachi singers and anyone else relying on tips to pay the rent. Marta's home was visited several times by Jesus of Nazareth, and she was known for her hospitality, so it is for that reason many in the service industry pray to her before they start their shifts at the restaurants. Maids pray to her so that they get tips from the houses they are going to go clean. She is prayed to when there are domestic problems, as well as called upon by sisters whose siblings are sick. A candle of Saint Martha can be found burning on a stove to keep everyone in the house safe from harm.

Santa Barbara also makes the top of the list, right under La Virgen de Guadalupe, in statues, candles, pendants, and more. Santa Barbara is kept in homes to keep evil away—or his ex-girlfriend as far away as possible! A young girl will light candles to her when love problems arise and ask to soften his heart and show him that she loves him. She prays to Santa Barbara when he gets together with "His Boys" to keep him safe. Because Santa Barbara was locked away in a tower by her father, many teenage girls also pray to her before they ask their parents if they can go out with a boy or out with friends.

Poverty is no stranger to the citizens of the East End. For this, the residents of the area turn to two saints: Saint Martin of Tours and Saint Jude. Saint Martin is prayed to by many to keep the poor safe; he is a protector to those who have no place to call home, the beggar on the street, the illegal who just arrived, the one who has no shelter, no identification and no place to call their own. We pray to San Martín Caballero (Saint Martin of Tours) to be a blessing to those on the streets; to clothe them with his heavy cape; to keep them safe from the cold. We petition San Martin to keep those who have no dwelling safe from the outdoor environments. We give clothes to the needy when we petition Saint Martin, or give change to the homeless, or help feed them at the local missions.

The Greater East End is known for their soup kitchens and free meal locations and food pantries—there is always an opportunity to volunteer and give back for your blessings. When food is low and the food stamps are depleted, they pray—turning to Saint Martin to provide food for their family: "San Martin, He always comes through." A young man tells me, "Lots of times we run out of food stamps, because it's hard with five kids, and my wife don't work cause she watching the two young ones at the crib."

Marcelo Garcia, a 26-year-old Hispanic, faithfully wears a bracelet with San Martin around his wrist. Pointing at it and making the sign of the cross he says, "It's hard, I don't want to be on welfare, and I work construction and cement. In the colder times it's a lot harder to find work. God puts these saints here for us, to help us." I ask him how it is that Saint Martin has helped him and his family. He tells me that when they run out of food stamps, they ask Saint Martin for help. Before they can become hungry, someone in the area is throwing a party and cooking a carne (meat)—everyone is invited to come eat, to celebrate.

Saint Judas Tadeo is the go-to saint for finances. San Judas is there to help when you are short on rent, utilities, or whatever bill you have. "You can ask everyone around for $20 to help pay the light bill, and no one's got it right? But when you ask Saint Jude, it's like, you don't even have to ask, you could find it on the floor in a parking lot or your tía happens to have it. He helps us man," says Heidi, a young lady with two kids living on Capital and 75th, "We put the bills under his feet when they come in." Putting the utility bills under his feet will control their spending and helps them in tight months. "We don't make no salary, man. Here, we get paid by the hour, and if boss man cuts our hours at work, it cuts our cash," says Mike. He and his girlfriend live across the hall from Heidi.

Saint Jude is rewarded with chocolates in gold foil, resembling the gold plate with the image of Jesus on it. He is given green pears and apples, as well. I was asked not to take pictures of the altar in the hallway of their small four-plex apartment.

Finally, there is one saint here who remains quiet. Tucked away in between rose bushes and flowers; Aloe Vera plants and Hibiscus bushes is Saint Francis of Assisi. Many know him for being the patron saint of animals, but here, Saint Francis is used in the gardens. "He brings peace and love to your home and makes your flowers bloom all year long," the old lady tells me in Spanish. This is Señora Lorenz who has lived on Navigation for 30 years, another main vein in the Greater East End, running right alongside of Harrisburg Street. "Yes, you see the dogs, Saint Francis keeps them in their yards. He keeps them safe when they wander in the streets or they escape to go look for the female."

Saint Francis, while the patron saint of animals, here is specifically used to keep dogs safe. The cheapest and most loyal of security systems in Latin Communities!

"You don't have to give him anything in return," says Señora Lorenz, crossing herself as she continues, "He had the marks of The Christ, his reward is greater than what you can give him. All you have to do is make a nice garden for the statue. So when he comes to visit, he has a pretty garden to sit in. He likes that."

The Greater East End is a world all on its own. She is tucked away, embraced by Highway 45 to the South, the 610 Loop to the East, and the Buffalo Bayou to the North. She is distinguished by her pastel colored homes, low-cost mechanic and tire shops, and guys pushing carts carrying traditional Mexican ice creams and snacks. Known for the best taco trucks in the city and home to thousands of working class Latinos, this part of Houston is deeply embedded with roots of Latin cultures living in the Greater East End. The Saints I discussed are just a hand full of spiritual entities that are prayed to and worked with here—the saints are also accompanied by Virgins and Angels of many sorts. If you ever get a chance to visit Houston and find your way to Harrisburg Street, just drive down. You will see the beauty that is Los Barrios de Houston.

Vela de Santa Barbara

For this work you need:

- Santa Barbara Glass Encased Candle, Red Wax
- Saint Barbara Oil
- Protection Oil
- Ground Eggshell (about two pinches)
- Jasmine Flowers (about two pinches)
- Two Cowry Shells
- Red Glitter
- Pink, Red & White Ribbon

Take the candle and load it with the two oils. Press the two cowry shells into the wax and sprinkle in ground eggshells, Jasmine flowers, and red glitter. As you sprinkle these in, speak to Saint Barbara and tell her what your need is. When you are done, tie the ribbons around the top of the glass and let it hang down the side of the candle. This candle is lit as soon as you can, there are no specific days to light candles. You will need to wash the area where you set the candle with Rose Water before you light it. Every day until the candle goes out, you will sprinkle rose water around the candle.

Vela de Santa Marta

For this work you need:

- Santa Martha Glass Encased Candle, Green Wax
- Saint Martha Oil
- Money Draw Oil
- Cloves (about two pinches)
- Hyssop (about two pinches)
- Green Glitter
- Green White and Yellow Ribbon

Take the candle and load it with the two oils. If using whole cloves, press those into the wax first. Sprinkle in the cloves and hyssop and green glitter, petitioning Saint Martha with your need. When you are done, tie the ribbons around the top of the glass and let it hang down the side of the candle. This candle is lit as soon as you can, there are no specific days to light candles. You will need to wash the area where you set the candle with Florida Water before you light it. Every day until the candle goes out, you will sprinkle Florida Water around the candle.

Vela de San Martin Caballero

For this work you need:

- Saint Martin Glass Encased Candle, Red Wax for Protection of Poor, Blue Wax for Food matters
- Protection Oil
- Allspice (About two pinches)
- Cats Claw (About two pinches)
- Purple, Gold, or Red Glitter (All three can be used)
- Blue, Yellow & Red Ribbons

Take the candle and load it with the two oils. Sprinkle in your Allspice, Cats Claw, and Glitter, petitioning Saint Martin of Tours with your need. When you are done, tie the ribbons around the top of the glass and let it hang down the side of the candle. This candle is lit as soon as you can, there are no specific days to light candles. You will need to wash the area where you set the candle with Kananga Water or Orange Blossom Water before you light it. Every day until the candle goes out, you will sprinkle Kananga Water or Orange Blossom Water around the candle.

About the author: *Oskar "Doc Mojo" Yetzirah is the Owner-Operator at Midtown Mojo Manufacturers, Host for Bayou City Conjure Radio at Local Live Media, LLC. and Outreach Coordinator at United States Veterans Initiative. He resides in Houston, Texas. He can be found on Facebook:*

https://www.facebook.com/bayoucityconjuredocktor

Latin American Folk Magic Conjure Oil Formulas

Protection Oil

- Hyssop
- Rue
- Allspice
- Olive Oil as a base

Money Draw Oil

- Cloves
- Lodestone
- Olive oil as a base

Creole Moon's Conjure Club

FOR THE SERIOUS STUDENT OF SOUTHERN CONJURE

If you are an information seeker, an academic interested in the inner workings of southern conjure traditions, or a practitioner of conjure yourself, you will love our Conjure Club. Each month you will receive on the average 3 to 4 digital downloads and ebooks full of information about traditional conjure workings, working with Catholic saints and folk saints, information about herbs and roots, conjure formularies, various spirits found on the altars of rootworkers all over the South, how to work with lamps, graveyard work, bottle spells, money magic, love spells and much, much more!

Our sources of information include word of mouth from real practitioners and elders, family, friends, and a variety of anthropological, folkloric and literary sources. The editor spends hundreds of hours locating and reading out of print books and journals, and compiling information from those sources, as well. Our downloads include references for students and for individuals seeking to broaden their knowledge base even further.

The core contributors for Conjure Club are people who were born and raised in the Southern United States, and who were immersed in conjure traditions as members of Southern culture. This gives us a unique perspective that can only be seen and experienced from within the culture. Our mission is to report on our experiences in an effort to preserve our cultural traditions. For more information, please visit:

www.creolemoon.com/conjure-club.htm